SCHOLASTIC
News
Nonfiction Readers

Jupiter

by
Christine Taylor-Butler

SCHOLASTIC INC.

New York Toronto London Auckland Sydney
Mexico City New Delhi Hong Kong Buenos Aires

W9-CBU-801

These content vocabulary word
builders are for grades 1-2.

Consultants: Daniel D. Kelson, Ph.D.
Carnegie Observatories
Pasadena, CA
and
Andrew Fraknoi
Astronomy Department, Foothill College

Curriculum Specialist: Linda Bullock

Photo Credits:

Photographs © 2005: Finley Holiday Films: cover, 2, 4 bottom left, 7, 23; Holiday Film Corp.: 5 bottom right, 13; NASA: back cover, 1, 4 top, 5 top, 5 bottom left, 9, 15, 17, 19; Photo Researchers, NY/Detlev van Ravenswaay: 4 bottom right, 11; PhotoDisc/Getty Images via SODA: 23 spot art.

Book Design: Simonsays Design!

ISBN 0-516-25060-4

12 11 10 9 8 7 6 5   6 7 8 9 10/0

Printed in the U.S.A.   08

First Scholastic paperback printing, October 2005

CONTENTS

WORD HUNT

Look for these words as you read. They will be in **bold**.

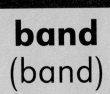

band
(band)

Jupiter
(**joo**-pih-tuhr)

solar system
(**soh**-lur **siss**-tuhm)

4

Europa
(yur-**oh**-pah)

Io
(**i**-oh)

space probe
(spayss prohb)

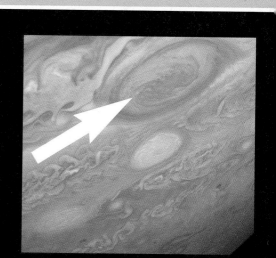

storm
(storm)

5

Jupiter!

Can you dance on **Jupiter**?

No. You cannot dance on Jupiter.

You cannot even stand on the planet.

Jupiter is made of liquids and gases.

There are lots of clouds on Jupiter.

They make the planet look like it has stripes.

The clouds form **bands** of color. They are blue, brown, yellow, white, and red.

The bands move in opposite directions.

The wind between them blows very fast.

On Jupiter, winds blow as fast as 240 miles per hour.

Jupiter is the fifth planet from the Sun.

It is the largest planet in the **solar system**.

All the planets rolled together could fit inside of Jupiter.

You could fit 1,400 Earths inside Jupiter.

Jupiter

Earth

Sun

Jupiter has many **storms**.

One storm is called the Great Red Spot.

This storm is two times wider than our whole planet.

This storm is like a hurricane on Earth. But it has lasted more than 300 years.

Great Red
Spot

Jupiter has more moons than any other planet.

There are 63 moons.

The moon closest to Jupiter is **Io**.

Io has many volcanoes.

A volcano is a mountain made of lava. Lava is hot liquid rock.

Io is about the same size as Earth's moon.

Europa is next to Io.

This moon looks very different from Io.

It is covered with ice.

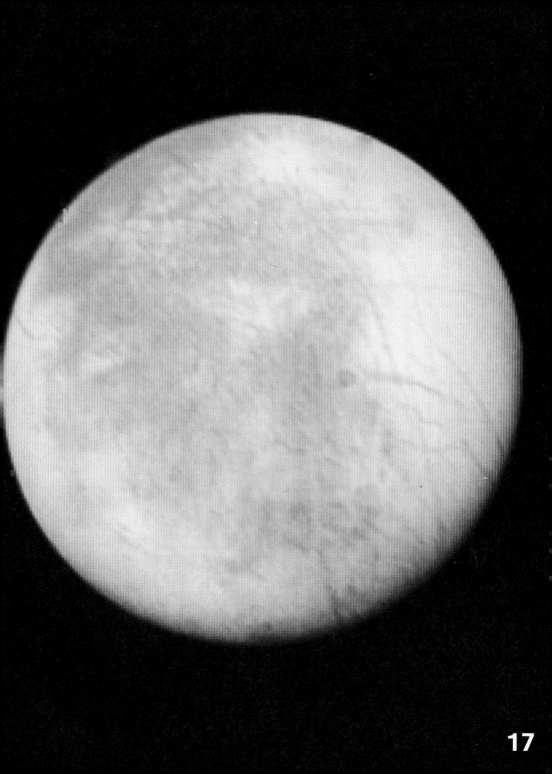

The **space probe** *Galileo* went to Jupiter.

In 1994, pieces of a comet hit Jupiter. *Galileo* sent us pictures.

In 2003 *Galileo* could do no more.

Scientists at NASA crashed it into Jupiter. They did not want it to hurt Jupiter's moons.

A space probe has no people in it.

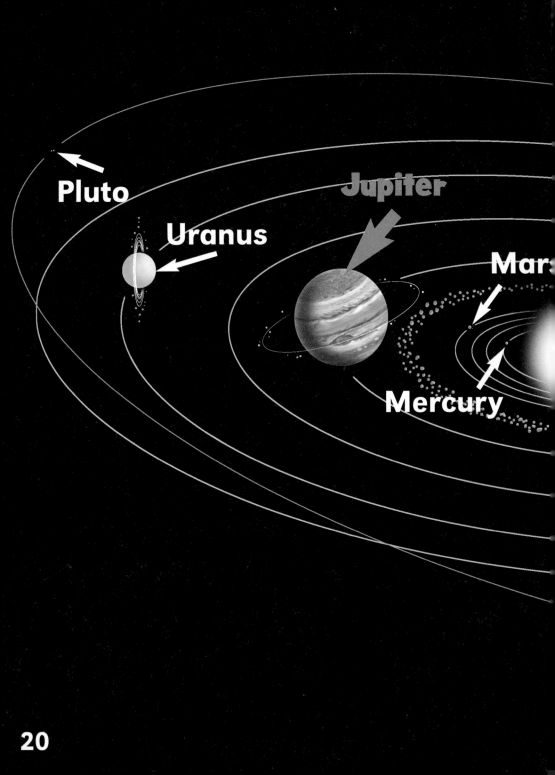

Pluto

Uranus

Jupiter

Mars

Mercury

20

JUPITER
IN OUR SOLAR SYSTEM

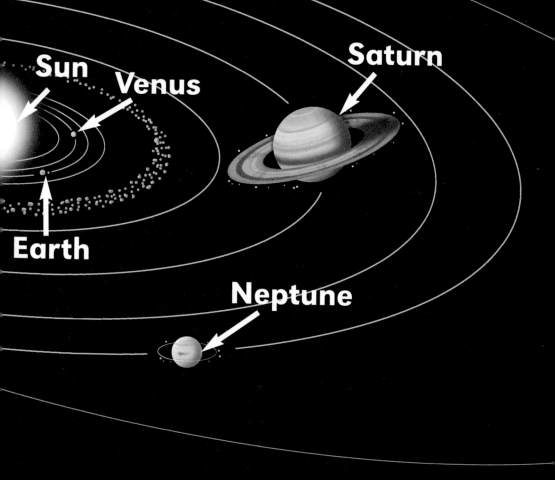

Sun

Venus

Saturn

Earth

Neptune

YOUR NEW WORDS

band (band) a long strip of clouds

Europa (yur-**oh**-pah) the second moon
of Jupiter

Io (**i**-oh) the first moon of Jupiter

Jupiter (**joo**-pih-tuhr) a planet named
after the king of the Roman gods

solar system (**soh**-lur **siss**-tuhm)
the group of planets, moons, and other
things that travel around the Sun

space probe (spayss prohb) a vehicle
with robotic equipment used to
explore space

storm (storm) heavy rain, snow, sleet, or
hail with strong winds

Earth and Jupiter

A year is how long it takes a planet to go around the Sun.

 **Earth's year
=365 days**

**Jupiter's year
=4,331 Earth days**

A day is how long it takes a planet to turn one time.

 **Earth's day
= 24 hours**

**Jupiter's day
= 10 Earth hours**

A moon is an object that circles a planet.

 **Earth has
1 moon**

**Jupiter has 63
or more moons**

**Did you know that
Jupiter is the fastest
turning planet in our
solar system?**

INDEX

FIND OUT MORE

Book:
Children's Atlas of the Universe
By Robert Burnham
Reader's Digest Children's Publishing, Inc., 2000

Website:
Solar System Exploration
http://sse.jpl.nasa.gov/planets

MEET THE AUTHOR:

Christine Taylor-Butler is the author of more than 20 books for children. She holds a degree in Engineering from M.I.T. She lives in Kansas City with her family, where they have a telescope for searching the skies.